Amish Cookbook:
Delicious, Fast and Easy Amish Recipes

By

Valerie Alston

Table of Contents

Introduction 5

The Secret Behind Amish Cooking 6

1. Amish Bread Recipes 8

2. Amish Dinner Recipes 16

3. Amish Dessert Recipes 26

4. Amish Country Favorites 33

5. Some Secret Recipes Revealed 39

Conclusion 43

Thank You Page 45

Amish Cookbook: Delicious, Fast and Easy Amish Recipes

By Valerie Alston

© Copyright 2014 Valerie Alston

Reproduction or translation of any part of this work beyond that permitted by section 107 or 108 of the 1976 United States Copyright Act without permission of the copyright owner is unlawful. Requests for permission or further information should be addressed to the author.

This publication is designed to provide accurate and authoritative information in regard to the subject matter covered. This work is sold with the understanding that the publisher is not engaged in rendering legal, accounting, or other professional services. If legal advice or other expert assistance is required, the services of a competent professional person should be sought.

First Published, 2014

Printed in the United States of America

Introduction

You may not know much about the people of Amish, their religion, customs or traditions but you must surely know about their food or would've at least heard someone raving about it. But before we talk about their food, lets first look at who the Amish are, for people who don't know.

The Amish are a separate and distinct part of the Traditionalist Christian Church whose roots stem from Swiss Anabaptist origins. Amish people can easily be identified in a group of people as even after so many years (and modernization) they have kept a simple lifestyle in which not only do they dress differently, but also their mode of transportation, their education, their attitudes, everything is different. Their dresses are plain and simple and usually of darker shades. The men adorn hats and beards, while the women adorn long dresses. But that's not what makes them most distinct. It's the fact that they have refused to adopt modern technology in any way. Whether it is electricity or kitchen appliances. And still their food is mouth watering, which in itself is quite an achievement.

The Secret Behind Amish Cooking

People who have had Amish dishes can vouch for the fact that there is something special behind each meal that they have had. But when you ask the Amish women what makes their food so special or whether they have some secret cooking tips, they just laugh it off insisting that there are no secrets or no special ingredients. Having said that it's still difficult to deny the special taste the Amish dishes have. Not only that but their food is way healthier too (and that is 1 reason for the Amish being much healthier than any other average person).

So what is it then? Well the answer lies in their lifestyle. The Amish have shunned modernism and technology, meaning that in their kitchens there is no place for packaged or preprocessed foods. So this means that everything the Amish use to prepare food is natural, organic and locally grown. Also they use a lot of healthy fats in the form of fresh butter and milk. All these things combined make Amish dishes extra healthy and extra delicious.

Amish Recipes

When you think traditional food, you must surely think Amish food as no one does traditional better than the Amish. Their meals are the epitome of home cooked grandma style meals and here we will share some of them.

1. Amish Bread Recipes

Amish Friendship Bread Starter

Used in so many other Amish recipes, so it is great to know how to make this.

Ingredients:

1 ½ cup plus 1 tablespoon of sugar

1/4th cup of warm water

1/4th ounce of a packet of yeast

3 cups of milk

3 cups all-purpose flour

Method:

The method takes a couple of days.

- Day 1

1. Take the 1 tablespoon of sugar, sprinkle it over the warm water and then sprinkle the yeast over this and

set aside for about ten minutes in a warm place till it doubles in size.

2. Now mix 1-cup milk, ½ cup sugar, 1-cup flour and the remainder of the yeast mixture in a bowl or container and stir with a wooden spoon. Then cover this loosely and let it stay in room temperature the whole night.

3. During this time the mixture rises to double and sometimes even triple its size.

- Days 2, 3 & 4

Keep the mixture loosely covered at all times and each day stir with a wooden spoon.

- Day 5

On the 5th day add 1-cup plain flour, 1-cup milk, and ½ cup sugar and stir once again and then loosely cover it up.

- Days 6, 7, 8 & 9

Do the same as you did from days 2 till 4.

- Day 10

Stir in the remaining cup of flour, ½ cup sugar and the 1-cup of milk and now your Amish friendship bread starter is ready for use. But if you are not going to use it straight away then either refrigerate it or freeze it.

Amish Friendship Bread

Make this classic Amish bread and blow away your friends and family.

Ingredients:

1-cup of Amish friendship bread starter

2 cups divided flour

2 cups milk

2 cups divided sugar

$2/3^{rd}$ of a cup of oil

1-cup sugar

1-teaspoon of vanilla

3 eggs

2 cups flour

½ teaspoon of baking soda

1 ½ teaspoon baking powder

½ teaspoon salt

1-teaspoon cinnamon

Method:

- Day 1

Leave the 1-cup of starter dough covered loosely in a warm place.

- Days 2, 3 & 4

Using a wooden spoon stir the starter dough once a day

- Day 5

To the starter dough add 1 cup of sugar and 1 cup of milk and stir well.

- Days 7, 8 and 9

Just stir the dough

-Day 10

1. Take 2 containers and add 1 cup of the mixture into each container. Take 1 cup for current use and refrigerate the other cup for future use.

2. Take the 1-cup of dough and to it add the oil, 1-cup sugar, the eggs, vanilla, baking soda, 2 cups flour, baking powder, cinnamon and salt. Mix well.

(Do make sure the oven has been pre-heated at 350 Degrees F)

3. Mix this well and have greased and sugared loaf pans ready to pour the mixture into.

4. Bake at 350 degrees F for forty-fifty minutes. Once done let it cool for ten minutes before removing them from the pans.

Amish Cornbread

An easy to make bread that goes well with soups and stews as a side dish.

Ingredients:

1 cup of Amish Friendship starter

1 ½ cups of milk

2 eggs

½ cup all-purpose flour

2 teaspoons sugar

1 ½ cup cornmeal

3/4th teaspoon baking soda

¼ cup vegetable oil

1-teaspoon baking powder

1/2 teaspoon salt

Method:

1. Preheat your oven to 425 degrees F and grease a 9-inch baking pan.

2. Take a large mixing bowl and to that add the starter, milk, eggs, flour, sugar and cornmeal and beat at the medium speed for 2 minutes.

3. Now mix in baking soda, oil, salt and baking powder.

4. Pour this mixture into your prepared baking pan and bake it at 425 degrees F for 25-30 minutes.

2. Amish Dinner Recipes

Try out these Amish dinner recipes for just yourself or whether you have a dinner party at home. These are so healthy and so tasteful. You will definitely start including more and more Amish dinner recipes in your meal times.

Simple Shepherd's Pie

This is an easy to make beef casserole, which will surely be a family favorite.

Ingredients:

2 pounds of ground beef

½ onion, chopped

Salt and garlic powder, up to taste

3/4th an ounce package brown gravy mix

2 cans cream of mushroom soup

2 ½ cups of water

1 ½ cups of frozen slice carrots, which have been thawed

10 Ounces package frozen peas, which have been thawed

Salt, pepper and paprika, up to your taste

2 ½ to 3 cups of potatoes which have been peeled, boiled and then mashed

Method:

1. Pre-heat your oven to 350 degrees F.

2. In a skillet, brown your beef with the onion and then add as much of the seasoning as you want. Afterwards drain it and pour it in to a large bowl.

3. Now stir in the gravy mix, soup, water and the vegetables. Mix well.

4.Trasnfer this in an already greased 9-inch deep-dish pie pan and sprinkle with a little salt and pepper.

5. Now take the mashed potatoes and spread them over the top of the mixture in the pan and then bake for 45 minutes at 350 degrees. Sprinkle with Paprika.

Amish Six-Layer Dinner

A casserole has always been an American dinner favorite dish. So what can be better than the six-layer casserole, which has 6 delicious layers including layers of hamburger and potatoes?

Ingredients:

2 cups of raw ground beef

2 cups of raw potatoes, washed, peeled and sliced

2 cups of celery, chopped

½ cup of onions, diced

2 teaspoons of salt or up to your taste

¼ teaspoon of pepper

1 cup of green pepper, diced

2 cups of canned tomatoes

1 medium onion

Method:

1. Pre-heat oven to 350 degrees F.

2. Grease a casserole dish of your choice.

3. Now add the layers in this order: At the bottom place the potatoes, then the celery, then the hamburger, then the onions and then the green pepper. On top of all of this pour the tomatoes. (Make sure to sprinkle salt and pepper after adding a layer.

4. Bake at 350 degrees F for 2 hours.

Spicy Oven Fried Chicken

Who doesn't like chicken? This recipe for spicy oven fried chicken will surely make you forget about KFC and its fried chicken which is packed with unhealthy preservatives. This on the other hand has no preservatives and is totally natural and healthy and would go well so with fries and coleslaw. This should be an instant hit with the family.

Ingredients:

1/3rd cup of vegetable oil

1/3rd cup of butter

½ cup of flour

½ cup of breadcrumbs

½ cup of yellow cornmeal

1½ teaspoons of garlic salt

1½ teaspoons of paprika

1-teaspoon of salt (or up to taste)

1-teaspoon black pepper (or up to taste)

4 pounds of chicken pieces, or any 14 pieces of your choice (such as thighs, breast halves, legs, wings)

Method:

1. Pre heat your oven to 375 degrees F.

2. Take a shallow pan and put the oil and butter in it and put it in the oven so that it melts. Then set aside.

3. Now take a large paper bag and to it add the flour, breadcrumbs, cornmeal and the seasonings.

4. Take the chicken pieces and one by one first roll them in the oil and butter mixture and then put them in the bag containing the flour and breadcrumb mixture. Shake the bag around until the chicken is well coated.

5. After you have coated all the chicken pieces, arrange them on an already greased oven tray. Make sure that the skin is on the bottom.

6. Bake for 45 minutes at 375 degrees F. After the 45 minutes have gone, carefully change the sides of the chicken so that the skin side is on the top now.

7. Now bake for a further 5 to 10 minutes or until the top crust starts to bubble.

Homemade Amish Chicken Pot Pie

No one does pies better then the Amish people and this Chicken Pot Pie is one of my personal favorites.

Ingredients:

1 ½ cup of flour

1 egg

½ onion, chopped

3/4th cup of peas

3/4th cup of milk

1-teaspoon salt

3 cups of chicken broth

2 carrots and celery sticks, diced

3 cups of chicken breasts, cooked and cubed

1/2-teaspoon parsley and pepper

Method:

- Soup base:

1. Take a pot and add all the vegetables to it and then cover it with chicken broth and add the parsley to it. Now add the seasoning up to taste.

2. Turn the flame to medium-low and simmer until the vegetables are tender.

- For Noodles:

1. Take a bowl and mix together the egg, salt, flour and milk. If you happen to find the dough a bit sticky, add more flour to it.

2. Sprinkle flour on your working area and roll out the dough onto it and cut 1 ½" squares from the dough to make noodles.

3. Add these squares to the soup base and cook on medium heat for another 10 minutes till the noodles are done.

3. Amish Dessert Recipes

Now that we've gone over some main course dishes, time to look at some great tasting, sugar filled, Amish desserts. Like all other Amish dishes, theses desserts too are healthier than the average dessert and taste just like homemade desserts should.

Shoofly pie

This pie is the perfect example of a typical homemade Amish desert and so quick and easy to make, that after you've made it once you will keep on making it again and again.

Ingredients:

1 cup of boiling water

1/2-cup of dark molasses

1/2-cup of light corn syrup

1 large egg, slightly beaten

1 1/2 teaspoon of baking soda

1 1/2 cup of flour

1/4th cup of butter

3 tablespoons sugar

3 tablespoons brown sugar

1/4th teaspoon cinnamon

1/8th teaspoon cloves

1 unbaked 9-inch pie shell (Put this into a heavily greased pie pan)

Method:

1. Pre-heat oven to 350 F.

2. To the boiled water, add molasses, corn syrup, egg and baking soda and let it stand for 15 minutes.

3. In another bowl, mix the remaining 6 ingredients and stir continuously with a fork until the mixture becomes crumbly.

4. Now divide the crumbly mixture into 2. Mix one half of the crumbly mixture with the molasses mixture and

pour it into the pie shell. Take the remaining crumbly mixture and cover the pie shell.

5. Place in oven and bake at 350 degrees F for 45 to 50 minutes.

Amish Strawberry Pie

This is an easy and quick dessert and is excellent for a dinner party or even on any normal day if you are a fan of strawberries.

Ingredients:

1 ½ cup of water

3/4th cup of Sugar

2 tablespoons of corn flour/cornstarch

3 tablespoons of strawberry gelatin

1-quart of fresh strawberries

1-teaspoon of lemon juice

Whipped cream for topping (if you want too)

A nine inch baked and prepared pie crust, which has been cooled

Method:

1. In a pan, boil together the water, cornstarch and sugar for one minute.

2. After one minute, take off the pan from the heat and add the lemon juice and gelatin and let it cool slightly.

3. After it has cooled a bit, add the strawberries and pour it into the already baked piecrust.

4. Serve with whipped cream.

Amish Sugar Cookies

These can be eaten any day of the year, but are huge hit around Christmas and Easter time.

Ingredients:

4 ½ cups of all-purpose flour

1-teaspoon of baking soda

1 cup of butter + 1 cup of vegetable oil

1 teaspoon of cream of tartar

1 cup of granulated sugar (+ some additional sugar for stamping) + 1 cup of powdered sugar

1-teaspoon of vanilla extract

2 eggs (large size)

Method:

1. Pre-heat your oven to 375 degrees F. Take an oven tray, line it with baking paper and then lightly grease the baking paper.

2. Take a large bowl and beat together the butter, sugars and oil until they are completely blended together and the mixture seems to be creamy. Now add the eggs and vanilla and beat it all again thoroughly.

3. Sift the dry ingredients together and then stir them into the mixture and make sure they blend in completely with the mixture.

4. Now take spoonfuls of the dough and drop it on the baking paper and then flatten each dough ball to a $3/8^{th}$ inch thickness using either a cookie stamp or the downside of a glass. (If you are going to be using a glass then make sure the bottom of the glass has been dipped in granulated sugar.)

5. Put the tray in the oven and bake the cookies at 375 degrees F for around ten to twelve minutes or up to the point when the edges start to brown.

6. Take out immediately then, so as to prevent them from over baking. Then let them cool a bit before serving. Served best with a cold tall glass of milk.

4. Amish Country Favorites

Now that we've gone over some Amish recipes of my choice, now let's look at some of the favorite recipes of the average person who has had Amish food. Again these recipes are quick, easy to make and so wonderfully delicious.

Amish Strawberry short cake

This Amish strawberry short cake will literally melt and crumble in your mouth. Such a great dessert combined with the awesomeness of strawberries. You will definitely want more of this.

Ingredients:

- For the shortcake:

2 cups of flour

4 teaspoons of baking powder

3/4th teaspoon of salt

1-tablespoon of salt

1-tablespoon of sugar

$1/3^{rd}$ cup of shortening

$2/3^{rd}$ cup of milk

1 egg (slightly beaten)

- For the topping:

½ cup of sugar

½ cup of flour

3 tablespoons of butter

- For the strawberries:

4 pounds of strawberries (cleaned and cut into 4)

Method:

1. Use the flour, baking powder, salt, sugar and shortening to make crumbs. Then to the crumbs add the milk and the egg and mix well until they are combined together. Spread this mixture into an already greased 8 x 8 cake pan and put this aside.

2. Now work on the top of the cake and for that mix together the flour, sugar and butter. This mixture should be crumbly and when you have reached that consistency, pour it over the mixture in the cake pan.

3. Now put in the oven and bake for 30 minutes at 350 degrees F. (But keep on checking after 35 minutes have passed by inserting a toothpick in the cake. It is ready if the toothpick comes out clean.)

4. During the time the cake is baking in the oven, prepare the topping. For this mix the strawberries with ½ cup of sugar. Put these in the fridge for around 3-4 hours so that they are cold and sweet afterwards. (You can also do this step earlier in the day if you want to serve the cake as soon as it comes out of the oven)

5. Once the cake is done and so are the strawberries, you can cut pieces from the baked shortcake and then layer it together with the refrigerated strawberries, as you like. In the end, you can add more of your favorite fruit, or whipped cream or ice cream on the top of the shortcake.

Amish Style Macaroni Salad

This is such a yummy and full of flavor salad. Not only that but it is extremely health as well and loved by both adults and children. A must starter for an Amish styled or for that matter any dinner party. Or will even go great for your child's birthday party.

Ingredients:

2 cups of elbow macaroni

3 stalks of celery, chopped

1 small onion, chopped

3 hard-cooked eggs, chopped

2 tablespoons of dill pickle relish

1 small carrot, shredded

1 small red bell pepper, take out the seeds and then chop it

2¼ teaspoons of white vinegar

2 cups of creamy salad dressing

White sugar to your taste (but in between 1/3 – ¾ of a cup)

¼ teaspoon of salt

3 tablespoons of prepared yellow mustard

¾ teaspoon of celery seed

Method:

1. Boil the macaroni with a little salt for around 8-10 minutes or until cooked. After they are cooked, rinse the macaroni with cold water and then let it drain and cool down.

2. Take a large bowl and stir in together the onion, macaroni, eggs, red pepper, celery, carrot and the relish.

3. Now take a small bowl and stir together the vinegar, sugar, salad dressing, salt, mustard and celery seed. (You can also add all these ingredients in a container and then shake the container to mix the ingredients together with each other.) Your dressing is now prepared and ready to be poured over the salad. After

pouring it, stir the contents of the large bowl so that the salad and dressing blend in together. Cover the bowl and put it in the refrigerator for at least an hour as this salad is served best cold.

5. Some Secret Recipes Revealed

The following three recipes are favorites of some of the Amish ladies as they have a particular technique to make them and also include some surprising ingredients in them.

Mashed Potatoes

I don't think there is anyone who can say no to mashed potatoes and how can you? I mean they are so creamy and yummy and go well with so many main course dishes such as steaks and fish. But what's so special about these mashed potatoes is that these will remain creamy no matter how long they have been prepared for or no matter the number of times you have re warmed them. And this is a great bonus as sometimes there are left over mashed potatoes but they don't taste that well the next time you re-warm them but in this case, when the mashed potatoes are re warmed they will see as if they were just freshly made.

This recipe serves 20 so you can adjust the recipe according to the number of people you have to make them for.

Ingredients:

10 pounds potatoes, (peel them and cut them)

4 ounces of cream cheese

½ cup of evaporated milk

$1/4^{th}$ cup of butter

½ cup of sour cream

1 tablespoon of salt (or up to taste)

Milk (as needed)

Method:

1. Boil the potatoes until soft and then mash them with a potato masher until they become fine.

2. To these add the cream cheese and mix well. Then add the butter and sour cream and again mix well.

3. Now add the milk for the consistency of your choice and then add salt up to your preference. Creamy mashed potatoes are now ready.

Easy Noodles

These noodles are also easy to make, but the best part about this recipe is that you never need to boil the noodles, they just becomes tender on their own. This is a great recipe for kids as usually kids love noodles.

Ingredients:

2 tablespoons butter

3/4th quart of chicken broth

3/4th cup of water

2 tablespoons of chicken base

Parsley

½ can cream of chicken soup

Salt (up to taste)

Any brand of noodles

Method:

1. Melt the butter in a saucepan until light brown and then the chicken broth, water, chicken base, parsley, cream of chicken soup and salt. Bring this to a full boil.

2. Add noodles of your choice in the mixture and instantly turn off the heat. Cover the pan and let it sit for around 45-60 minutes. During this time the noodles will become tender and you will have your own homemade version of instant noodles minus all the preservatives and additives that are in the instant noodles sold at supermarkets.

Conclusion

You may have tried many cuisines from throughout the world but once you will try Amish food, nothing will beat that. Their traditional, home-cooked meals are out of this world and will always keep you coming back for more and that is why it is no wonder why Amish restaurants have such long queues outside their restaurants. Though what surprises me the most is that Amish are present in such a small population and still their food is so popular.

The popularity of their food is due to the home grown, natural ingredients they use and also the fact that do not use any packaged or pre-processed food. So everything being prepared by them is fresh and we all know that nothing beats fresh home cooked meals. This is a reason why most people refer to Amish cooking as 'grandmother styled cooking'. And there is no doubt in that as the different blend of flavors in the Amish dishes are proof of how much hard work goes in making one dish. Though the actual preparation and cooking time for dishes may not be that much, but the time and effort taken to grow and collect all those natural ingredients going in their dishes is priceless.

And this shows in the taste and appearance of their food, breads and desserts. So you may or may not have yet experienced any Amish recipes, but trust me when I say this, that once you do, you will see a lot more Amish dishes in your daily routine. Because not only are they healthy and tasteful but for you they are also quick and easy to make and will be an instant success with your friends and family.

Thank You Page

I want to personally thank you for reading my book. I hope you found information in this book useful and I would be very grateful if you could leave your honest review about this book. I certainly want to thank you in advance for doing this.

www.ingramcontent.com/pod-product-compliance
Lightning Source LLC
LaVergne TN
LVHW011154050225
803025LV00005B/140